Also by Sarah A. Chrisman:

First Wheel in Town
Love Will Find A Wheel
A Rapping at the Door
Delivery Delayed

Victorian Secrets
This Victorian Life
True Ladies and Proper Gentlemen
Love's Messenger
Words for Parting

A Christmas Wish

Victorian Winter Poetry for Christmas and New Year's

Compiled and edited by
Sarah A. Chrisman

Contents

Introduction…p. 9

Joys of the Season…p. 12
December…p. 13
Winter Is Coming… p. 14
The First Snow…p. 15
Sleigh-Bells…p. 17
Gingerbread…p. 19
The Cranberry Tart…p. 20
Popping Corn…p. 21
The Skaters…p. 22
A Winter Morning…p. 24
The Sleigh-Ride…p. 26
The Mistletoe…p. 30
A Christmas Glee…p. 32
Choosing the Mistletoe…p. 34
Christmas Greens…p. 36
The Mistletoe Bough…p. 37
A Christmas Song…p. 39

Eager Anticipation… p. 41
The Day Before Christmas…p. 42
What Willie Wants…p. 44

The Christmas Pretender...p. 45
Santa Claus's Birds...p. 47
Dear Santa Claus, Come!...p. 48
A Letter To Santa Claus...p. 50
Will He Come?...p. 52

Merry Christmas!... p. 55
Christmas Morn...p. 56
Christmas Chimes...p. 57
Christmas on the Farm...p. 59
A Christmas Greeting...p. 61
Joy to the Christmas Time...p. 62
Christmas Day...p. 64
Christmas Land...p. 66
Christmas Pensées...p. 67
Our Christmas...p. 68
An Old Aunt's Gift...p. 71
A Christmas Wish...p. 72
A Christmas Party...p. 73
Baby's Christmas Gift...p. 78
Baby Joe's Philosophy...p. 79
Grandma's Christmas, Too....p. 80
A Christmas Wish...p. 82
December...p. 83

Happy New Year!... p. 85
Elsie and the Year...p. 86
The Coming of the New Year...p. 87

What the New Year Brings…p. 89
Watching for the New Year…p. 91
Another Year…p. 92
The Old and the New…p. 96
Welcomes and Adieus…p. 98
We Forget Hours But Remember Moments…p. 99
The New Year…p. 101
The Dawning of the Year…p. 102
At The New Year Morn…p. 103
January…p. 104
1890…p. 105
A Coasting Song…p. 107

Introduction

The winter holidays connect past and present. The months of frost and snow are a natural time to tend our hearths and tell stories of prior ages, and the long nights of winter are perfect for dreaming about them. To the Victorians Christmas was an especially nostalgic time, with tales of yule logs and renewed but ancient traditions of holly boughs and mistletoe. At the same time people were reviving old traditions they were adopting new ones. Queen Victoria's husband Prince Albert introduced German Christmas trees to Britain, from whence they traveled to America. The Christmas gift-giving tradition as we now know it was born with the burgeoning consumer culture of the late nineteenth-century, and it has certainly thrived ever since.

Right on the heels of Christmas comes New Year's and January —a month named after the old Roman god who examined past and future simultaneously. It is a time to be grateful for the treasures of the past, and to invest those treasures, in the form of wisdom, in our dreams for the future.

The poems in this collection were copied from Victorian family magazines

which were collectively read and enjoyed by cheery firelight on long winter nights in the nineteenth-century. They brought friends and families together in the coziness of home and in shared celebration. Their power and ability to do this has not faded over the years. May they bring you and yours much joy and the blessings of the season.
    Happy holidays!
    —*S.C.*

Joys of the Season

December

Though in her pride young June may wear
A rose wound in her shining hair,
Yet will the gem of Christmas rest
Upon December's snowy breast.

—Lucy C. Kellerhouse
The Ladies' World, December, 1896, p. 19.

Winter Is Coming

A windy sky—
Brown branches swaying.
A russet carpet of fallen leaves;
No more shall I,
Through green fields straying,
Cull the sweet flowers that Nature weaves.

A slim new moon
In the ether sailing,
Frosty and keen is the evening air;
A song I croon
Of the winter, hailing
Its bracing pleasures and Christmas care.

The curtain drawn,
The logs pile higher,
We'll welcome the friends that we love so well;
The winds may roar
Till they redden the fire,
Then ho! For the stories we love to tell.

—Ione L. Jones
Good Housekeeping, December 10, 1887, p. 75.

The First Snow

Sunset

Over meadows, brown and sere,
Creeping on
Comes the slowly waning year;
Wood and lawn
Dreary look, but holding still
Something of Dame Nature's will.

For the autumn's golden dress,
Lying low,
May have lost its gaudiness,
And the flow
Of the brook sounds strangely drear,
With the waning of the year.

Mocking-bird and woodland thrush,
Passed away,
May have left a lonely hush
In the day,
And the golden-rod may rock,
In the breeze, a crownless stock;

But, I pray you, look once more,
For the ground
Is a white and fluffy floor,

While around
Everything is crowned with snow.
Autumn's final overthrow.

Deep the sun, in yonder haze,
Lightly floats;
Looking on earth's quiet ways.
Heaven notes
Its fair purity, for hush,
Lo, the earth reflects her blush.

—Walter M. Hazeltine
Good Housekeeping, December 6, 1890, p. 377.

Sleigh-Bells

Do you hear the merry bells,
Defiant, wild, and gay?
How their ringing joy dispels
The gloom of life away!

Ringing, dancing, on they come,
Enticing those within—
Tasks and books away therefrom—
With their persuasive din.

"Ding-a-ling, a-ling, a-ling!"
The stars come and and laugh;
"Laugh away!" The sleigh-bells ring,
"We don't do things by half."

See the horses toss their heads,
The snow-balls, —how they fly!
Upward thrown, as each steed treads
The snow, so crisp and dry.

Youthful voices from the sleigh
Commingle with the rhyme;
Sleigh-bells, laughter, speed away,
Enjoy it —now's the time.

Ponies, shake your jetty manes;

My lasses, spend your wit;
Dash away o'er hills and plains,
The queen of night has lit.

—M.R.M.
Godey's Lady's Book and Magazine, December, 1873, p. 538.

Gingerbread

Mary Hanner, run this minute;
Get the pail, with 'lasses in it;
Fetch the shortn'nin' and the flour.
Hurry, —don't be gone an hour!
Bring the salt and soda, —hear me?
Bring the pans, and put 'em near me.
We must never have it said
Mary Hanner Perkins wed
'Fore she l'arnt her gingerbread.

Run and fetch your mother's glasses.
There! Now look; a cup o 'lasses;
Next a tablespoon of lard,—
Stir it in and beat it hard;
Now a little drop o' water—
Get it at the pump, my da'ter;
Now dissolve the soda in it;
One egg whipped for half a minute;

Pinch o' salt; now sift your flour in.
There! Take care —you've got a power in!
Stir it, beat it, whip it, —see!
Light and right as dough can be.
Where's the ginger? That's well thought on;
Strange it was so nigh forgotten!
Without that it can't be said
Gingerbread is ginger-bread!

—Ida Whipple Benham
Good Housekeeping, December 24, 1887, p. 95.

The Cranberry Tart

All honor to the Cranberry Tart,
And her who fashioned thee at will,
O rarest work of plastic art!

What memories at thine image start,
How didst thou once our senses thrill?
All honor to the Cranberry Tart!

Awhile fond glances would we dart
Ere we thy sweets would wanton spill,
O rarest work of plastic art!

Each gazer fond, with all his heart,
Would then fall to, and eat his fill,
All honor to the Cranberry Tart!

Our adolescent loves depart;
But haply thou canst please us still,
O rarest work of plastic art!

Though newer viands, dishes smart,
Invite with Gallic name and skill,
All honor to the Cranberry Tart,
O rarest work of plastic art!

—Anonymous
The American Kitchen Magazine, December, 1898, p. 89.

Popping Corn

Just when the room is getting dark
And the night wind whistles low,
The children gather around the fire
All in a merry row.
Noon's the time for the bubbles light,
And tops may spin at morn,
But just when the twilight shadows fall
Is the time to pop the corn.
See it! Hear it! Pop! Pop! Pop!
Hippity! Skippity! Hop! Hop! Hop!
Dolls and hoops may do for morn,
But night's the time to pop the corn.

Golden grains in your hands you hold,
But into the pan they go,
And quick as a wink the wizard Heat
Will turn them all to snow.
Shake them up with a steady hand
Over the firelight bright,
Then turn them out into the big brown bowl
In their fluted caps of white
See them! Hear them! Pop! Pop! Pop!
Hippity! Skippity! Hop! Hop! Hop!
Kites and tops may do for morn,
But night's the time to pop the corn.

—Angelina W. Wray
The Ladies' World, December, 1896, p. 14.

The Skaters

And in the frosty season, when the sun
Was set, and, visible for many a mile,
The cottage windows through the twilight blazed,
I heeded not the summons: happy time
It was indeed for all of us; for me
It was a time of rapture! Clear and loud
The village clock tolled six —I wheeled about,
Proud and exulting like an untired horse
That cares not for its home. All shod with steel
We hissed along the polished ice, in games
Confederate, imitative of the chase
And woodland pleasures, the resounding horn,
The pack loud-bellowing, and the hunted hare.
So through the darkness and cold we flew,
And not a voice was idle: with the din
Meanwhile the precipices rang aloud;
The leafless trees and every icy crag
Tinkled like iron; while the distant hills
Into the tumult sent an alien sound
Of melancholy, not unnoticed, while the stars,

Eastward, were sparkling clear, and in the west
The orange sky of evening died away.

Not seldom from the uproar I retired
Into a silent bay, —or sportively
Glanced sideway, leaving the tumultuous throng,
To cross the bright reflection of a star,
That gleamed upon the ice; and oftentimes,
When we had given our bodies to the wind,
And all the shadowy banks on either side
Came sweeping through the darkness, spinning still
The rapid line of motion, then at once
Have I, reclining back upon my heels,
Stopped short; yet still the solitary cliffs
Wheeled by me —even as if the earth had rolled
With visible motion her diurnal round!
Behind me did they stretch in solemn train,
Feebler and feebler, and I stood and watched
Till all was tranquil as a summer sea.

—Anonymous
Winter pictures by poet and artist, 1882, pp. 154—155.

A Winter Morning

The keen, clear air —the splendid sight—
We waken to a world of ice;
Where all things are enshrined in light,
As by some genie's quaint device.

'Tis Winter's jubilee —this day
His stores their countless treasures yield;
See how the diamond glances play,
In ceaseless blaze, from tree and field.

The cold, bare spot where late we ranged,
The naked woods, are seen no more;
This earth to fairy land is changed,
With glittering silver sheeted o'er.

A shower of gems is strewed around;
The flowers of winter, rich and rare;
Rubies and sapphires deck the ground,
The topaz, emerald, all are there.

The morning Sun, with cloudless rays,
His powerless splendour round us streams;
From crusted boughs, and twinkling sprays,
Fly back unloosed the rainbow beams.

With more than summer beauty fair,

The trees in winter's garb are shown;
What a rich halo melts in air,
Around their crystal branches thrown!

And yesterday! —How changed the view
From what then charmed us; when the sky
Hung, with its dim and watery hue,
O'er all the soft, still prospect nigh.

The distant groves, arrayed in white,
Might then like things unreal seem,
Just shown a while in silvery light,
The fictions of a poet's dream;

Like shadowy groves upon that shore
O'er which Elysium's twilight lay,
By bards and sages feigned of yore,
Ere broke on earth heaven's brighter day.

O God of Nature! With what might
Of beauty, showered on all below,
Thy guiding power would lead aright
Earth's wanderer all Thy love to know!

—Anonymous
Winter Pictures by Poet and Artist, 1882, pp. 130—131.

The Sleigh-Ride

Over the snow, over the snow,
Like a shaft let loose from an archer's bow,
Like a deer on the foot, when the hunters are nigh,
Like a bird on the wing, when the fowler is by,
Like the rush of a stream when its frost-fetters break,
Like the surging of billows when tempests awake,
Like the crash of an avalanche quitting its place,
Like a red-streaming meteor careering through space,
Like the sweep of the whirlwind when forests are bowed,
Like the flash when the thunderbolt leaps from its cloud,
Like the swoop of the eagle as he darts on his prey,
Like the message the lightning speeds forth on its way,
With a wild sense of freedom exulting we go,
Over the snow, over the snow.

Bear away! For our comrades are drawing too near;
Be alive, man, and horse! Lest we fall in the rear;
To your speed, Bucephalus! The van is our place!
Hurrah! We have won! And we lead in the race.
I knew that not one of their coursers in speed
Could match for a moment our mettlesome steed.
Clear the track! Is the word, as we dart on our way,
And inanimate objects the mandate obey;
The farmhouses wheel to the left and the right,
And stupidly stare as we vanish from sight;
The fences fall back, and the trees stand aside,
And make way, with a will, for our hurricane ride,
As on like a band of wild huntsmen we go,
Over the snow, over the snow.

How the stars wink and laugh as they watch our mad course
And the moon gravely quizzes each rider and horse;
Laugh away! In your orbits celestial you go,
Much faster than we, on our planet below.

Then the girls —bless their hearts— how their
sweet voices ring,
Like the gushing of bird notes that welcome
the Spring!
Bright-eyed! Cherry-lipped! Oh, 'tis glorious
to ride
With the girl that you love nestled close to
your side!
While you talk in low tones —for the others
are near,
And the dear little head bends closer to hear
The whisper that sends the soft cheek all
aglow,
Under the rose and over the snow.

What a volume of melody surges and swells
Abroad on the air from our musical bells!
The clash of the cymbals, the clarion's breath,
The trumpet that summons to glory and death,
The peal of the organ where censers are
swinging,
The harp of the minstrel through lordly halls
ringing,
The blast of the bugle where squadrons are
wheeling,
The strain of a lute on the charmed air
stealing,
Are less sweet to the ear than the ocean that
swells

In the rhyme and the chime of our musical bells.
And life seems more glorious, humanity dearer,
The heart, hand, and brain, warmer, firmer and clearer,
And our pulses keep time with our bells as we go,
Over the snow, over the snow.

—Claire Crofton
Frank Leslie's Monthly Magazine, December, 1876, p. 692.

The Mistletoe

With Christmas cheer the hall is bright,
At friendly feud with winter's cold;
There's many a merry game to-night
For maids and men, the young and old;
And winter sends for their delight
The holly with its crimson glow,
And paler than the glistening snow
The mistletoe, the mistletoe.
The mistletoe! The mistletoe!
The wan and wanton mistletoe!

Chance comer to our festal eyes,
Dear crimson-breasted holly-sprite!
Thee, Robin, too, the hall receives,
Unbidden, whom our hearts invite.
And perched among the crumply leaves,
He cocks his head and sings, Hullo!
The mistletoe, the mistletoe
Hangs up above, but what's below?
Oh! What's below the mistletoe?
The mistletoe, the mistletoe!

A kindly custom sanctions bliss
That's ta'en beneath the wanton bough.
Who laughs so low? Why, here it is!
Look, Jenny, where I have you now!

Dear bashful eyes! Sweet lips —a kiss!
Ah! Cheeks can mock the holly's glow!
   For what's below the mistletoe?
    Ah! Ha! Why, it is Cupid O!
   Ah! Ha! Below the mistletoe
   'Tis Cupid O! 'Tis Cupid O!
—H.C.
Temple Bar. January, 1893, p. 22.

A Christmas Glee

Come, haste, let us seek it,
The dear Christmas holly—
Its crimson lights gleam brightly forth from the snow;
See it reach out its bonnie green boughs as an offering—
A rare Yule-tide gift on its friends to bestow!

Go seek it, ye children,
The dear Christmas holly—
Seek it first for the home-shrine with swift, loving hands;
Bring its sheen and its glow to the place made most sacred
By tears and by joys, throughout kingdoms and lands.

Go seek it, ye yeomen,
The brave Christmas holly—
Make a forest of emerald and red in the kirk—
Bring the rarest of sprays for the altar—and to it
Come, worshipers, all—be ye Christian or Turk.

Go seek it, ye skeptic,
The dear Christmas holly—
As you clasp this bright emblem of Yule-tide—forsake
Your scorn of the truth and your grim speculations,
And of the deep joy of the Yule-tide partake.

So gather it, good folk,
The dear Christmas holly,
Let it glow from the altar, and shine at the feast—
May the glory and love of the Christ-child surround us
As shone the light down from His star in the East!

—Helen Chase
Good Housekeeping, December 6, 1890.

Choosing the Mistletoe

'Twas Christmas Eve, and all the land
Had donned a robe of spotless white,
When through the orchard, hand in hand,
We went amid the waning light.
For you had left the cheerful town,
And walked a mile across the snow,
To hold the apple branches down,
And help me choose the mistletoe.

Each tempting bough with frost was wreathed;
The creamy berries grew so high,
They shone like pearls in silver sheathed
Against the brightness of the sky.
It must have been the sunset red
Which lent my cheeks that crimson glow,
As, softly o'er my drooping head,
You —held a spray of mistletoe.

The glory of the west grew pale
And faded to a primrose bar;
Grave Twilight dropped her misty veil,
And clasped it with a diamond star.
The chimes rang out for Evensong
Before we thought 'twas time to go:
It always seems to take so long

When *two* must choose the mistletoe.

Since then, the years have rolled away,
And other lips sweet stories tell;
And other lovers stroll to-day
Adown the path we loved so well.
Dear heart, old memories make me weep,
But you —you only smile to know
That with Love's dearest gifts I keep
A withered spray of mistletoe.

—E. Matheson
Chamber's Journal, December 13, 1890, p. 800.

Christmas Greens

Bring ye boughs of spicy pine,
Wreathe the ivy's clinging vine,
Spruce and hemlock to the sense
Like the Magi's frankincense,
Bring ye in the holly green,
With the berries' scarlet sheen
Laurel fit for hero's brow,
Fragrant box bring hither now:
All that winter frost doth spare
In our joyous feast may share,
Bough and berry, leaf and vine
We will offer at His shrine
Who for us in time of old
Left his glories manifold,—
Left His Kingdom, left His Crown,
And in pitying love came down,
Here a little child to be
Cradled in humility.

—Albie F. Judd
Good Housekeeping, December 25, 1886, p. 73.

The Mistletoe Bough

They are hanging the Mistletoe, bonny and bright,
A spray in the parlor, a wreath in the hall;
My children, I watch them, and wonder tonight
Why Alec and Alice are growing so tall.
'Tis only a day since their stockings they hung,
And begged for a story at bedtime, but now
They're dreaming of lovers, their comrades among,
And kisses, I ween, 'neath the Mistletoe Bough.

I close the door gently, come back to my place,
The firelight is falling so softly across
The fender, I fancy it outlines a face;
My heart hurts anew with the sense of its loss;
While memory retraces, as oft in the past,
The time since that eve, when I pressed on the brow
Of my shy little sweetheart, unchallenged at last,
A tender 'troth kiss 'neath the Mistletoe Bough.

Life's for love, love is life, and the years were so blest,
The years that I kept her, my bonny-faced bride;
World-weary at last, to the Country of Rest,
She folded her hands, and went out with the tide.
My children, I need you, I'm lonely to-night.
Come sit by my side while I tell again how
The yule log was burning, the holly was bright,
When I first kissed my love 'neath the Mistletoe Bough.

—Lalia Mitchell
Good Houskeeping, November, 1894, p. 238.

A Christmas Song

Heap the holly! Wreath the pine!
Train the dainty Christmas vine—
　Let the breath of fir and bay
　Mingle on this festal day—
　Let the cedar fill the air
　With its spicy sweetness rare.
Wake the carol —sound the chime—
Welcome! Merry Christmas time.

　Bring the fronds of hardy fern—
　Let the Christmas berries burn
　Mid the sprays of richest green;
　Weave the ivy's polished screen;
　And the radiant Christmas rose
　　In gray mistletoe enclose.
　Snowy fleece and sparkling rime
　Welcome! Merry Christmas time.

From some sunny forest knoll
Bring the Yule log's mighty bole;
Where the pine's weird music make
There the storied Yule tree take.
Spread the board with rare good cheer—
　Hail the fête day of the year.
Wake the carol —sound the chime—
Welcome Merry Christmas time.

—Helen Chase
Good Housekeeping, December 26, 1885, p. 93.

Eager Anticipation

The Day Before Christmas

It is so tempting to know they're there—
I will not peek in, though I truly could—
Heaps of toys, and the door unlocked,
Such a chance to go in, and some boys would!

Last night the expressman brought a load,
And up the stairs, at the end of the hall,
To the little room —it must be full—
Nurse and Papa carried them all.

I think —I'm sure that there is a drum
And a sled, and I hope there's a music box,
I want one more than anything else,
And I saw the baby's new picture blocks;

And Gracie's muff, that came with her skates;
And Nellie's doll, it is tall as herself;
I was trusted to know so much —and books
For Ned and Jim, they're there on the shelf.

I've painted a picture of baby Nell
Holding her doll, it is most life size;
I'm the family artist —I'll be one yet—
There's something the matter with the eyes;

And the head isn't quite right on the neck,

But to make a live girl's picture, oh, my!
It's a hard thing to do and have it like,—
    If you don't believe it, why, just try!

I painted the picture for Mamma;
    And didn't I work —it took a week!
Oh! How can I wait for Christmas Day?
    But a boy of honor wouldn't peek.

It makes me laugh to see them jump
When a fellow comes into the sitting-room;
To-day Grace hid her work in her lap,
I saw, she was making a case for a broom.

My whisk, I didn't let on, not I!
And I've seen —if they knew they'd be shocked.
I guess I'll go up there and guard that door;
Ha! There's no temptation now —it's locked!

—Mrs. M.F. Butts
Good Housekeeping, December 25, 1886, p. 80.

What Willie Wants

Dear Santa Claus:
You brought a sled
To me a year ago;
And when you come again I hope
You'll bring along some snow.
—Willie

—"Willie"
Saint Nicholas Magazine, December, 1891, p. 96.

The Christmas Pretender

When Christmas time is almost here,
And folks begin to wink,
And hush their talk when I come near,
Then I begin to think
I'll write to Santa Claus about
The things I want, to fill
My stockings. —He won't get the note,
But I pretend he will.

I slip it in the envelope,
And put it with the mail,
And beg Mamma to send it
By the postman, without fail;
And thank her when I find it gone,
For doing what I bid;
I know she never sent it off,
But I pretend she did.

I take my stockings Christmas eve,
And by the chimney side
I hang them, while I wish that they
Were twice as long and wide;
And wonder how the chimney
Lets him down, that jolly man!
Of course I know it truly can't,
I pretend it can!

And when on Christmas morning,
All the things I wanted so,
Are sticking from my stocking tops,
Or standing in a row,
I hug and kiss my mother,
And my father, too, because
I know it's mostly them, though I
Pretend it's Santa Claus!

—Mrs. George Archibald
Good Housekeeping, December, 1896, p. 256.

Santa Claus's Birds

Dear Santa Claus keeps a bower of birds
To carol his Christmas glees,
And every year their joyous notes
Resound through the Christmas trees.

Good Santa's birds are children dear,
They keep our hearts in tune,
And mind us of a better world
As roses tell of June.

Oh! What a dreary world this were,
How barren, bleak and cold,
If childhood's harmless mirth were hushed,
If all the young were old.

Then blessings be on Santa's birds,
And blessings on their lays,
For childhood is a glimpse of heaven,
Is sunshine of our days.

—Carine L. Rose
Good Housekeeping, December 22, 1888. p. 81.

Dear Santa Claus, Come!

Dear Santa Claus, come!
The clock has struck one,
And all in the house are in bed;
The stars brightly glisten,
We'll not peep nor listen,—
Our stockings are hung overhead.

A cup of hot tea
In the kitchen you'll see,
A pie and a plate of cold meat;
And a pailful of oats,
Such as reindeer or goats,
If tired and hungry, would eat.

I know you will come
From your ice-palace home,
Your nose frost-bitten and red,
Your reindeer a-prancing,
Your sleigh-bells a-dancing,
A jaunty fur cap on your head,

With all sorts of toys
For good girls and boys,
And presents to hang on the tree;
With cakes, nuts and bon-bons,
Made for the little ones,

And brought from over the sea;

Doll babies that talk,
And lap-dogs that walk,
Jumping-jacks, whistles and whips,
Muffs, gloves and mittens,
A ball for the kittens,
And slippers with bright bead tips.

A sword and a drum
For Corporal Bumm;
For papa, a nicely bound book;
A Punch and Judy
For mimicking Ruby,
And something to suit the cook.

For Mamma please bring
A large diamond ring,
And an elegant sealskin sack;
And for little Sadie
(You know she's the baby),
All that is left in your pack!

—Frank H. Stauffer
Good Housekeeping, December 25, 1886, p. 83.

A Letter To Santa Claus

Dear Santa Claus, please don't forget to call at our house
Our little kids will watch for you, each "quiet as a mouse;"
Unless the sand man comes too soon and shuts some blinking eyes
That wait the coming reindeer sleigh from out the wintry skies.

There's Tom, and Ben, and Sue, and Kate, and little blue-eyed brother,
And me, but I'm the oldest one, so 'bout me don't you bother;
If Tom could have a painted sled, and Ben could have a top,
When one gets tired of using his, why, they could make a swap;

If Sue could have a pretty doll, and Kate could have some dishes,
Our toddling brother have a book, with painted birds and fishes;
And if it ain't against your rule, to sometimes think of others,
I want to tell you that we have the very best of mothers.

One year ago our father died, and left us in the keep
Of God in heaven, and every night, before we go to sleep,
We kneel at mother's knee and say, "Father who art in Heaven;"
And mother whispers tenderly, "Let us all be forgiven."

So Santa Claus, if you will be to us so kind and good,
Please fill the smallest stockings first, and then if you but would
Skip mine and leave some little gift for loving mother dear,
We'll have a welcome Christmas day, though Father is not here.

A merry day for Tom, and Ben, and Sue, and Kate,
Tho' a green and fresh-made wreath will hang above the open grate,
And little brother, when a man, will thank you, with the rest,
That you did not forget to come, a welcome Christmas guest.

—Clark W. Bryan
Good Housekeeping, December 6, 1890, p. 376.

Will He Come?

Three pairs of little stockings,
"By the chimney hung with care;"
Three little elfs, each saying,
"Saint Nick will soon be there."

Three pairs of little, pattering feet,
Going boldly off to bed,
Where mysteries and visions
Fill full each little head.

Three little night-clad cherubs,
Stealing softly down the stairs;
Forgetting, in their curious haste,
To say their morning prayers.

Three little voices shouting,
"Oh! Santa Claus *did* come."
And Merry Christmas echoes swell
Throughout a happy home.

—Clark W. Bryan
Good Housekeeping, December 22, 1888, p. 87.

SANTA CLAUS, GOING HIS ROUNDS.

Merry Christmas!

Christmas Morn

Small feet before the dawn of day
Are marching to and fro;
Drums beat to arms through all the house,
And penny trumpets blow
A health to brave old Santa Claus,
And to his reindeer bold,
Whose hoofs are shod with eider-down
Whose horns are tipped with gold!

—Anonymous
Arthur's Illustrated Home Magazine, January, 1880, p. 52.

Christmas Chimes

Ring! Ring!
Christmas Chimes!
Holly shines on sheltered bills,
Snow the cedar thicket fills,
Through the world a message thrills—
"Peace, good will to men."
Ring, through all the leafless land;
Chime, where hut or mansions stand,
Christendom with outstretched hand
Yule-tide greets again.

Ring! Ring!
Christmas Chimes!
Mistletoe's rare olive sheen,
Clasps the fir's fringed branches green.
In the heavens the Star serene
Shines in blessing down,
Beams with holy light, to show
To the restless tide below
Peace and gladness forth—for so
Heaven its own shall crown.

Ring! Ring!
Christmas chimes!
Yule fires glow from hearth and hall,
Lights gleam out from torches tall,

Ringing carols round us fall,
Mirth and gladness reign;
Christmas joy be yours, good friends
Holly bough with palm-spray blends,
And His peace, the Christ-child sends
Through his fair domain!

—Helen Chase
Good Housekeeping, December 22, 1888, p. 76.

Christmas on the Farm

Skirting close the frozen brooklet, with its mirror face of ice
Are the willows with their tinkling bells a-merry in the morn,
The winds they softly waft on wings the songs of paradise,
And the snow-crust glistens brightly in the early sun that's shorn
Of its gleam and glow and glister, by the nodding hemlock trees
Spreading high their graven branches to the golden lights that kiss
The stumps, like cowled monks kneeling lowly on their bended knees;
Such is dawn of Christmas morning on the farm —and children's bliss.

Hear the prattle of the youngsters, as they tumble from their beds,
Eyes awide and hearts so eager, scarce can wait to great the feast;
Hamper-scamper down the stairway, rosy cheeks and curly heads,
Baby blossoms all, God bless them! We could spare not one at least.

Presents—who can name or count them?
Dolls and drums and pretty things
To make happy all our babies, make them
merry with delight.
How they chatter with sweet voices; how the
music echo brings
Gentle thrills of sweetest rapture to the
mother heart so bright.

—H.S. Keller
Good Housekeeping, December 22, 1888, p. 81.

A Christmas Greeting

I wish a merry Christmas
To every home on earth;
May lowly cot, may palace hall
Re-echo genial mirth.
May children's laughter gaily ring,
And happy voices gladly sing
A fond and joyous welcoming
To merry, merry Christmas!

I pray a holy Christmas
May come to every heart;
A time of sweet tranquility
From troublous care apart.
An hour for thoughts to soar above,
For heart to realize the love
And grace divine that, like a dove,
Brood o'er this holy Christmas.

God send a blessed Christmas
To every patient life;
A little resting from the toil,
A surcease from the strife.
May Faith breathe words of gentle cheer
Hope point to roses blowing near,
And tender love and friends sincere
Make this a blessed Christmas!
—Claudia Tharin
Good Houskeeping, December, 1894, p. 248.

Joy to the Christmas Time

Make glad to-night, O hearts, O hearts,
Beat to the glorious song,
That over the wintry hilltops
Is surging and swelling along.
That down in the depths of the valley
Throbs out all its wonderful tune,
'Tis a dream that will never be over—
Told again 'neath the silent moon.

O mother, draw closer your wee ones
And whisper in each tiny ear,
The angels' sweet, musical story
Ringing out so triumphant and clear.
O tell of the white light shining
Far brighter than radiant morn,
How it fell on the wondering shepherds
When the little Lord Jesus was born.

O tell of the wise men's journey
How afar from the East they came,
To offer their gifts and to worship,
And to call the blessed infant by name
How they bowed their heads in the brightness,
O softly the angels now sing,
They were masters of truth and of wisdom,
And they knelt to the baby King.

The stars shone pure in the heavens,
There was gladness and peace on earth,
There was bliss in that midnight hour
    O'er the little Lord Jesus' birth.
And to-night we hear the bells ringing
    With an echo in every chime,
Just a whisper of love o'erflowing,
And joy to the Christmas time.

—L.R. Baker
Godey's Lady's Book, December, 1889, p. 469.

Christmas Day

Though rude winds usher thee, sweet day,
Though clouds thy face deform,
Though Nature's grace is swept away
Before thy sleety storm;
Even in thy sombrest wintry vest,
Of blessèd days thou art most blest.

Nor frigid air nor gloomy morn
Shall check our jubilee;
Bright is the day when Christ was born,
No sun need shine but He;
Let roughest storms their coldest blow,
With love of Him our hearts shall glow.

Inspired with high and holy thought,
Fancy is on the wing;
It seems as to mine ear it brought
Those voices carolling,—
Voices through Heaven and Earth that ran,—
"Glory to God, good-will to man!"

I see the Shepherds gazing wild
At those fair Spirits of light;
I see them bending o'er the Child
With that untold delight

Which marks the face of those who view
   Things but too happy to be true.

Oft as this joyous morn doth come
   To speak our Saviour's love,
O, may it bear our spirits home
   Where He now reigns above!
That day which brought Him from the skies
   So man restores to Paradise.

Then let winds usher thee, sweet day,
   Let clouds thy face deform;
Though Nature's grace is swept away
   Before thy sleety storm,
Even in thy sombrest wintry vest,
Of blessèd days thou art most blest.

—Samuel Richards
Fulton and Trueblood's Choice Readings, 1884, pp. 134—135.

Christmas Land

Who has the key of Christmas Land?
Where the bonfire shines,
And the holly twines,
Carollers sing —a merry band—
And stars are bright o'er that fair strand—
Who has the key of Christmas Land?

Light are the hearts in Christmas Land;
In each group you meet
There are faces sweet.
Bosoms young and guileless are there,
And brows not yet wrinkled with care—
Who has the key of Christmas Land?

Dear baby hearts in Christmas Land,
We want to be near,
And join in your cheer
When the tree with its strange fruit bends,
And you wait for what Santa sends—
Who has the key of Christmas Land?

Love has the key of Christmas Land.
Oh! Come, Cherub Love,
With wings like the dove,
Spread over hearts thy light of peace,
Sow for a harvest full of increase—
Open the gates of Christmas Land.

—William Lyle
Good Housekeeping, December 6, 1890, p. 384.

Christmas Pensées

'Tis Christmas, merry Christmas,
With its holly-berries bright,
With its sweet and joyous carols
Chiming out into the night.

'Tis Christmas, happy Christmas,
With its greetings, when we hear
Pleasant sounds of salutation
And good wishes for the year.

'Tis Christmas, hallowed Christmas,
With its hidden sigh that tells
Of the shadow that hath fallen
Since the ringing of the bells.

'Tis Christmas, blessed Christmas,
With its memories untold,
Bringing joy and pain commingled,
As in Christmas days of old.

—Josephine Canning
Good Housekeeping, December 6, 1890. p. 373.

Our Christmas

We didn't have much of a Christmas
My Papa and Rosie and me,
For Mamma'd gone out to the prison
To trim up the poor pris'ner's tree;
And Ethel, my big grown-up sister,
Was down at the 'sylum all day
To help at the great turkey dinner,
And teach games for the orphans to play.
She belongs to a club of young ladies
With a "*beautiful objick*" they say,
'Tis to go among poor lonesome children
And make all their sad hearts more gay.

And Auntie, you don't know my Auntie?
She's my own Papa's half-sister Kate,
She was 'bliged to be round at the chapel
'Till 'twas, —Oh some time *dreadfully* late
For she pities the poor worn out curate:
His burdens, she says, are so great,
So she 'ranges the flowers and music
And he goes home around by our gate.
I should think this way *must* be the longest,
But then, I suppose he knows best,
Aunt Kate says he intones most splendid;
And his name is Vane Algernon West.

My Papa had bought a big turkey
And had it sent home Christmas Eve;
But there wasn't a soul here to cook it,
You see Bridget had threatened to leave
If she couldn't go off with her cousin,
(He doesn't look like her one bit)
She says she belongs to a "union"
And the union won't let her submit.
So we ate bread and milk for our dinner,
And some raisins and candy, and then
Rose and me went downstairs to the pantry
To look at the turkey again.

Papa said he would take us out riding—
Then he thought that he didn't quite dare
For Rosie'd got cold and kept coughing;
There was dampness and chills in the air.
Oh the day was *so* long and so lonesome!
And our Papa was lonesome as we;
And the parlor was dreary —no sunshine,
And all the sweet roses, —the tea,
And the red ones, and ferns and carnations
That have made our bay window so bright,
Mamma'd picked for the men at the prison;
To make their bad hearts pure and white.

And we all sat up close to the window,
Rose and me on our Papa's two knees,
And we counted the dear little birdies

That were hopping about on the trees.
Rosie wanted to be a brown sparrow;
But I thought I would rather, by far,
Be a robin that flies away winters
Where the sunshine and gay blossoms are.
And Papa wished he was a jail bird,
'Cause he thought that they fared the best;
But we were real glad we weren't turkeys
For then we'd been killed with the rest.

That night I put into my prayers,—
"Dear God, we've been lonesome to-day
For Mamma, Aunt, Ethel and Bridget
Every one of them all went away.—
Won't you please make a club or society,
'Fore it's time for next Christmas to be,
To take care of philanterpists' fam'lies,
Like Papa and Rosie and me?"
And I think that my Papa's grown pious,
For he listened, as still as a mouse,
Till I got to Amen; then *he* said it
So it sounded all over the house.

—Julia Walcott
The Ladies' Home Journal, December, 1887.

An Old Aunt's Gift

Many long, long years ago
Upon a Christmas day,
Among a wealth of gifts received
A tiny package lay.
It was so very, very small
It scarce had caught my eye;
So modest that, the truth to tell,
I near had passed it by.

A scented pin-ball lay within
The wrapper coarse and brown;
And with it in a shaking script,
The lines a-running down,
A little, neatly folded note
This message had to tell:
"Dear laddie, tho' the giftie's small,
Ye ken I love ye well."

Ah, that was long, long years ago,
I cannot now recall
A single costly gift that lay
Beside that scented ball.

—T.W. Burgess
Good Housekeeping, December, 1900, p. 344.

A Christmas Wish

Christmas ever comes love-laden,
Prompting wishes kind and true;
From my heart, O gentle maiden,
Here is one for you.
Like the rose of summer weather,
With a thousand beauties rife,
May all virtues blend together
In your happy life.

—Anonymous
A Crown of Flowers, 1883, p. 88.

A Christmas Party

Trim up the parlors, Goodwife, and make them extra-gay;
I'm going to have a party, on this cold Christmas day;
The friends that are invited will be here —do not doubt!
I'll go myself and bring them, if they don't come without.

Yes, you have been a-guessing, perhaps a month or two,
About *my* Christmas party, and what I meant to do;
The first whose invitations have been left all to me:
You're not quite sure concerning the guests you're going to see.

Our children? No, not this time; they've children of their own,
Whose Christmas trees are bending with presents newly grown;
They've got their life-vines planted, with love-flowers all about—
Just what *we* worked so hard for, when first we started out.

Our cousins? Well, not this time; 'tisn't what the plan intends;
They're all quite earthly-prosperous, with any amount of friends;
The world is always offering success an upward hitch;
But Christmas wasn't invented entirely for the rich.

Our preacher and his family? —They're working now, like sin,
A-sorting out the slippers and other gifts sent in;
One turkey that I know of is on their kitchen-blaze;
A cheery, popular preacher has good times, now-a-days!

You don't know who you've cooked for? —Well, that *is* most too bad;
Of course you've no cur'os'ty—no woman ever had!
But, still, your hands and heart, wife, have well nigh gone to war;
A woman works much happier, when she knows who it's for.

I'll tell you one: a cripple that you and I both know,
Is living in a small hut, half-buried in the snow—
His body bravely struggling to coax his soul to stay;

I'm going to get that cripple, and keep him here all day.

And one's a poor old woman we've never called our friend,
But whose sad life grows heavy while struggling to its end—
Without a merry Christmas for twenty winters drear;
To-day she'll have a pic-nic to last her all the year.

And one's an old-style preacher; brim-full of heavenly truth,
Whose eloquence lost fashion, or ran off with his youth;
And younger men and prettier, with flowery words came nigh;
And so the various churches have stood the old man by;

He tried his best to please them and serve Jehovah too—
He toiled each separate Sunday to "get up something new;"
They wanted elocution; and curvey-gestured speech;
And now this grand old preacher can't get a place to preach.

But I've a strong opinion, that angels crowd up near
That man-deserted leader, his God-like thoughts to hear;—
We'll have a Bible-chapter made over good as new,
When he to-day talks Gospel, and asks the blessing too!

"And who else?" —I have sent word to all in my mind's way,
Who can't afford a dinner that's equal to The Day;
And some good prosperous friends too, will come with smiling face,
To keep those poor from feeling that they're a separate race.

And one of them's a neighbor; who, though sincere, no doubt,
Once couldn't quite understand me —and so we two fell out;
And every Sunday morning we've passed each other's door,
And have not known each other for fifteen years or more:

I went to him last evening, and said, Old friend, see here;
We're both tip-top good fellows: now doesn't it strike you queer,

That we're assisting Satan to sow the grains of strife?
Come over, sure, to-morrow, and bring along your wife.

"Just come and help us, helping some poor ones draw their loads,
Who've stalled upon the side-hills of Life's uneven roads."
He looked at me in wonder—then stood a moment still—
Then grasped my hands, and whispered, "My dear old friend, I will."

I think you're with me, Goodwife, from what your features say;
And that's the kind of comp'ny we're going to have to-day—
Through which I hope a true love for all mankind may roam;
A sort of Christmas party where Christ would feel at home.

—Will Carleton
The Ladies' Home Journal, December, 1887.

Baby's Christmas Gift

What shall we give to the baby,—
Our baby just one year old?
She wouldn't know about Christmas,
Not even if she were told.

You may hang up her little stockings
Where Santa will surely see,
Or put all sorts of playthings
Upon the Christmas tree,—
But what does she know about Santa
And his wonderful midnight ride,
Or the tree that bears such fruitage
Only at Christmas-tide?

She'd only look in wonder
From out her big, blue eyes,
And reach her hands for the playthings
With innocent surprise.

So kisses sweet without number,—
Kisses and love untold—
These we will give to the baby,
Our baby, just one year old.

—Carrie W. Morehouse
Good Housekeeping, December 10, 1887, p. 71.

Baby Joe's Philosophy

Our Benny's new skates are a treasure,—
Patent clamped, nickel-plated, and bright.
Old Santa knew what would give pleasure
When he filled Benny's stocking that night.

Benny keeps them quite dry, and well polished
With chamois and pumice and oil,
Baby Joe watches all, much astonished;
Ben explains: "Lest they rust, Joe, and spoil."

Baby Joe in the air, keen and wintry,
With breath wreathed in clouds by the frost,
Cries, "My lips! Dry them quick, Brudder Benny,
'Cause, you know, if you don't, they will *rust*!"

—Josephine C. Goodale
Good Housekeeping, December 24, 1887, p. 87.

Grandma's Christmas, Too.

Little, bright-haired, thoughtful Florence
Half past four years old,
Had been waiting long for Christmas,
With its joys untold,
Firm believer in Old Santa,
Doubts crossed not her mind,
He would bring the things she wanted,
"'Cause he was so kind,"

"What do you suppose, now, Mamma,
Santa Claus will bring?
I guess I want a nice new dolly,
Most of anything;
And some books with lots of stories,
Or some building blocks,
Like those of Uncle Burt's, you 'member,
In a wooden box."

Now this little maiden, Florence,
(Like most maids of four)
Had a good, indulgent grandma,
Whom she did adore;
Often had she wished to see her,
In her distant home,
Oft-repeated was the question,
"When will Grandma come?"

Laughingly we asked the girlie,
"Wouldn't it be nice,
If Santa Claus should drive his reindeer
Over snow and ice,
Bring your grandma down here quickly,
Think a moment, dear,
Would you rather have him leave her,
Or some presents, here?"

In a moment came the answer
We scarce thought to hear:
"I would rather he'd bring Grandma,
With his eight reindeer;
But" —a shadow crossed the child-face
Looking into mine—
"He will bring some presents, won't he,
Next year, Christmas time?"

Ah, the grandmas! They're the loved ones
Of our childhood days,
Ever are their dear hearts planning
How to smooth our ways.
Wisely chose the little maiden,
Better than she knew
More than all the gifts, it brightened
Grandma's Christmas, too.

—Mabel Potter Tallman
Good Housekeeping, December 22, 1889, p. 91.

A Christmas Wish

Had I power to give to you
Many a rich and costly gem,
Fit, in brilliancy of hue,
To adorn a diadem,
I'd bestow the jewels rare
On some other friend less dear,
While for you I'd breathe a prayer,
Such as I do offer here.

Many a merry Christmas, friend,
Health, contentment, joy and bliss;
More delights in thought I send
Than I can convey in this.
With the now departing year
May your cares and sorrows cease;
May the new one, drawing near,
Bring you happiness and peace.

—S. Conant Foster
Outing and The Wheelman, 1883, p. 292.

December

The music of the brook is hushed,
Its restless motion stilled;
The leaves are faded, fallen, crushed,
The air with frost is filled;
The leafless trees look strange and lone,
And wildly toss their arms and moan.

The black-bird's notes of sturdy cheer
From out the tree-tops ring;
To drape the earth the clouds draw near,
A fleecy garment bring.
And wrapped in folds of purest white,
We bid the dear old year "Good-night."

—Sarah E. Howard
Good Housekeeping, December 8, 1888, p. 65.

Happy New Year!

The Coming of the New Year

How does the sylvan year begin
In woodlands gray and old?
Oh, icy winter shuts it in,
And laps it round with cold!
Then tarry yet a little, hasty year!
For, prithee, what of promise would you find?
Empty branches, wrenched asunder,
Muffled winds in mellow thunder,
And the sap flowing slower in the rind,—
Slow, slow lagging in the rind!

How does the sylvan year begin
By hill and pasture dun?
Their snowy billows glimmer in
The red light of the sun!
Oh, tarry yet a little, happy year!
What of pledge, what of promise would you find?
Lonely marshes, pale and sallow,
Windy field and frozen fallow,
And the earth unrelenting to her kind,—
A hard, hard mother to her kind!

How does the sylvan year begin
While yet the suns are brief?
The pledge of spring is folded in

The embryonic leaf!
Then come, for we wait you, joyful year,
And the life of the future you shall find!
Burrowing creatures without number,
Heavy in Arcadian slumber,
And the sowing of the forest on the wind—
The seed of the birches on the wind!

—Dora Read Goodale
Outing and The Wheelman, 1884. p. 279.

What the New Year Brings

The snow lies white on hill and dell,
The streams, with ice are closing fast,
The wind sweeps through the leafless trees,
The good old year has gone at last.

The fires are kindled on the hearth,
The lamps of eve are all alight,
As the western sky grows dark anew,
And stars come thick, this winter night.

The sleigh bells tinkle on the breeze,
The coaster speeds him down the hill,
The skater sweeps in graceful curves,
In the sheltered valley by the mill.

Without the air is cold and keen,
Within our home is bright and warm,
And pleasant pastime rules the hour,
What reck we then of cold or storm?

New Year, with joy we welcome you,
Although you come with breath so cold;
We greet you with our warmest smiles,
And meet you as we did the old—

In rounds or seasons, year by year

A herald each of coming spring,
Anticipating gladdened hours,
In springtime and its blossoming.

So as in life the seasons come,
So as in death the seasons go,
So hope will come in winter hours,
With promise bright of summer's glow.

—Anonymous
Good Housekeeping, January 1896, page 34.

Watching for the New Year

I.

The passing bell, for the dying year,
Rings through the silence far and near,
With solemn dirge-notes, soft and low
Tolling a requiem, sad and slow,
For swiftly passing Time!
Dying! Dying! Dying!
Ring out the bells in mournful rhyme!
Flying! Flying! Flying!
As we watch from the window the cold snow lying,
As white as the locks of Old Time.

II.

Hark! Far away in the old church-tower,
The clock is striking the midnight hour!
Merrily now ring out the bells,
Filling the air with joyous swells,
To greet the new-born Time!
Ringing! Ringing! Ringing!
Thrilling the world with her mirthful chime,
Merrily ringing,
The birth of a New Year, so joyously singing,
As we watch for the young, brave Time!

—George Weatherby
Peterson's Magazine, December, 1876, p. 408.

Another Year

"Time cuts down all, both great and small,"
And fruit when ripe is sure to fall.
Another year of labor and recompense has birth,
Another year of living, and all that life is worth,
Another year of hopes and fears, with many unfulfilled,
Another year of beating hearts that will ere its close be stilled.

Another year of mortal birth, of marrying and death,
Another year of error's ways, of sadly wasted breath,
Another year of noble deeds, of welcome words and ways,
Another year of pain and plaint, of songs and hymns of praise.

Another year of progress, of preaching, and of prayer,
Another year of politics, brazen, bold and bare,
Another year of mountebanks, of ridicule and show,

Another year of "Gallagher," and bids to "let him go."

Another year of sharp finance, and of feeble financiers,
Another year of scientists, and scientific sneers.
Another year of journalistic wit and wisdom brains,
Another year of rolling out their tongues and taking pains.

Another year of folderol, and funny-man nonsense,
Another year of pictures bold, and literary pretense,
Another year of scribbler's ink taking on pretentious airs,
Another year of the "new woman" coming down the stairs.

Another year of the man who waits, and wilts, and weeps,
Another year of the other one who never stops nor sleeps,
Another year of blatent bores, who boast of brains and brawn,

Another year of darkened souls, longing for the "dawn."

Another year of faithlessness, of fraud and froth and folly,
Another year of merriment, of mirth and being jolly,
Another year of gloom and grief, of sorrow, and the sad,
Another year of goodness, of glory, and the glad.

Another year of cycle wheels, with motorcycles coming,
Another year of jokes about rich plumbers and bad plumbing,
Another year of "witty" mother-in-law recital,
Another year of stealing brains without making a requital.

Another year of electrical trolley rails and lightings,
Another year of international rights, and wrongs, and writings,
Another year of fancy foreign fun and interference,
Another year of racing yachts, with talks of fouls in clearance,

Another year of tennis, golf, horse-racing and baseballs,
Another year of finding out the curse of "puts and calls,"
Another year of "corners" close in oil, in wheat and flour,
Another year of patent ways for making fortunes in an hour.

Another year of waiting for what it finds and brings,
Another year of many unknown and unthought-of things,
Another year of looking for what is not yet here,
Another year of birth, of brief being, and a bier.

—Anonymous
Good Housekeeping, January, 1896, p. 1.

The Old and the New

"Ah, my life is sweet," moaned the gray Old Year,
"And fleeting as the sere and yellow leaf."
"Hail! I come to reign," cried the bright New Year,
"And *all* the years do find dominion brief."

"Who art thou?" Coldly queried the Old Year,
"Usurper! Upstart! Dressed in vestments fine?"
"Keep thy temper, brother!" Laughed the New Year,
"For ancient styles are somewhat past their prime."

"You've dethroned me!" Crossly said the Old Year.
"My broken sceptre in the dust may stay."
"We'll put it by," slyly laughed the New Year,
"To rest (and rust), momento of thy day!"

"My heart is broken!" Sighed the Old Year,
"Memories rise to taunt me, bitter, sad."
"Nay! They offer dole," whispered the New Year,
"While I with joys arise full-sized and glad."

Toll the bells, mournfully, for the Old Year;
   Snows, gently bequeath him a pall!
Glad chimes ring merrily for the New Year,
   Which smiles a fresh hope for us all!

—Lydia Wood Baldwin
Good Housekeeping, December 6, 1890. p. 370.

Welcomes and Adieus

A welcome for the New-born Year,
And for the Old adieu,
Who outward goes with memories dear,
Of joy and grief, of pain and cheer,
While the infant comer, with promise bright,
With rosy cheeks and brow bedight,
With well-digested horoscope,
Filled with elements of earnest hope,
We bid the Old adieu,
And welcome, then, the New.

—Anonymous
Good Housekeeping, January, 1896, p. 5.

We Forget Hours But Remember Moments

They come to us —they come to us,
Point after point alone,
These little spots in memory,
Some moments we have known,
As flies the flashing lightning
From the dark unnoticed cloud,
Some moment bursts from years behind,
With magic power endow'd.

They come —they come: sad memories,
Dim moments let them stay,
They are partings, they are death scenes,
Do not hasten them away.
Tears, they bring you tears of sorrow,
But they bring you soothing too,
Whispering they are glorious beings,
Whom on earth as frail you knew.

They come, too: black remembrances,
How oft in hours of pride,
Before this idol self the sins
Of other years will glide.
Oh! Drive them not too soon away,
Nor let them tarry long,
Pray that their humbling ministries,

Make thy spirit strong.

Like a drop of rich aroma,
From the rose long since decay'd,
Like the light the star illumines,
When the earth is wrapped in shade;
Come some moment memory loveth,
Some delightful music strain,
Round the troubled spirit playing,
Rousing it to hope again.

Moments come —they are but moments,
When the raptured soul inspired,
Rose through earthly clouds and vapors
With celestial ardor fired.
Such with nought can we compare them,
Here alone description fails,
They are apertures whence shineth,
Heavenly light through earthly vales.

Present moments —let us use them
As if memory stored them all,
And so live that no dark folly,
Cunning memory may recall.

—H.W. Payson
Peterson's Magazine, January, 1853, p. 31.

The New Year

Only a garland of withered leaves;
Only the wail of the wind, that grieves
Over the dying year.
Sadly we listen; our hearts are full,
As we stand on the year's dim verge to cull
All memories sweet and dear.

As the sunset's flush in the western skies
Deepens in splendor as daylight dies,
So the glow of the holy-tide
Touches with lingering grace
The fading smile on the old year's face —
The face it has glorified.

Under the garland of withered leaves,
Lulled by the wail of the wind that grieves,
Is sleeping spring's fairy-train;
And gayly its ladder of stars there climbs
The musical peal of the New Year's chimes,
Bringing hope to our hearts again.

—Helen Marion Burnside
Peterson's Magazine, January, 1888, p. 58.

The Dawning of the Year

Another year!
Out of the mists and darkness of the night,
The new year comes with hope and holy light.
The glad bells chime the tidings of the morn—
"A year, a year, a golden year is born!"
Then all the fleeting shadows fade away,
And 'mid the old year's twilight, dim and gray,
I listen to the faithful bells that ring,
And wish that every heart might wake and sing.

Another year!
So full of hope and trust the soul should be,
So glad to feel a new-born energy.
Yet those there are who tread the old-time ways,
Remembering the griefs of vanished days.
Give such sad hearts, O Lord, Thy balm and cheer,
And let them taste the joy of this new year;
The way is light; the happy bells now ring,
And every heart should gladly wake and sing.

—Charles Handson Towne
The Ladies' World, January, 1896, p. 7.

At The New Year Morn

Fear held my hand as the Old Year passed
At dead of night, at dead of night.
White was the mantle about him cast,
And white was the spectre that held me fast.

Deep bells were tolled as the Old Year fled
At dead of night, at dead of night.
And I had thought of him lying dead
Where the snows beat down on his hoary head.

Hope drew me close when the New Year came
At break o' day, at break o' day.
Scarce would my lips speak her hallowed name;
The other had covered my heart with shame.

Glad was the watcher, his vigil o'er
At break o' day, at break o' day.
Fair were the tokens the morning bore,
And love entered in at his open door.

—Frank Walcott Hutt
The Ladies' World, January, 1896, p. 5.

January

January, crisp and clear,
First glad month of all the year,
Diamond crowned, a clasp of gold,
Holds in place her mantle's fold.
On her feet are tiny bells,
How their merry music swells;
Hood of snow and heart of fire,
In her hands a magic lyre.
Comes she thus our hearts to cheer,
Gayest month of all the year.

—Ruth Raymond
The Ladies' World, January, 1896, p. 4.

1890

With song and laughter welcome to our lands
The youngest born of Time —the glad New Year!
The people of the earth with outstretched hands
And eager hearts, give greeting: not one tear
Shall dim his birth! He comes to us a King—
Clothed in royal garb of hope and love,
While in his train fast follows each rare thing
Which dowers man with happiness —to prove
That life is bright and joyous, true and good
Despite the storms which oft disturb its flood.

Then Bells, chime merrily —ring him in cheerily,
He is blithesome and bonnie and dear,
And while ye are pealing our hearts will be feeling
That the hearts of our loved ones are near.
Ring in the North —and summon ye forth
The friend by his deeds confessed;
Ring in the South —for the sweet warm mouth
Of the woman we love the best.
Ring in the East —and the New Year's feast
Shall make the land its own;

Ring in the West —the Pacific's breast
  Re-echoes each joyous tone!

> —Lee C. Harby
> *The Ladies' Home Journal*, January, 1890, p. 4.

A Coasting Song

From the quaint old farm-house, nestling warmly
'Neath its overhanging thatch of snow,
Out into the moonlight troop the children,
Filling the air with music as they go,
Gliding, sliding,
Down the hill,
Never minding
Cold or chill,
O'er the silvered
Moon-lit snow,
Swift as arrow
From the bow,
With a rush
Of mad delight
Through the crisp air
Of the night,
Speeding far out
O'er the plain,
Trudging gayly
Up again
To where the firelight's
Ruddy glow
Turns to gold
The silver snow.
Finer sport who can conceive

That that of coasting New-Year's Eve?
Half the fun lies in the fire
That seems to brighter blaze and higher
Than any other of the year,
As though his dying hour to cheer,
And at the same time greeting give
To him who has a year to live.
'Tis built of logs of oak and pine,
Filled in with branches broken fine;
It roars and crackles merrily;
The children round it dance with glee;
They sing and shout and welcome in
The new year with a joyous din
That rings far out o'er hill and dale,
And warns the watchers in the vale
'Tis time the church bells to employ
To spread the universal joy.

Then the hill is left in silence
As the coasters homeward go,
And the crimson of the fire-light
Fades from off the trodden snow.

So the years glide by as swiftly
As the sleds rush down the hill,
And each new one as it cometh
Bringeth more of good than ill.

—C. Graham
Harper's Young People, December 30, 1879, p. 73.

Index of Titles

Another Year…p. 92
At The New Year Morn…p. 103
Baby Joe's Philosophy…p. 79
Baby's Christmas Gift…p. 78
Choosing the Mistletoe…p. 34
Christmas Chimes…p. 57
Christmas Day…p. 64
Christmas Glee, A…p. 32
Christmas Greeting, A…p. 61
Christmas Greens…p. 36
Christmas Land…p. 66
Christmas Morn…p. 56
Christmas on the Farm…p. 59
Christmas Party, A…p. 73
Christmas Pensées…p. 67
Christmas Pretender, The…p. 45
Christmas Song, A…p. 39
Christmas Wish, A ("Christmas ever comes love-laden…")…p. 72
Christmas Wish, A ("Had I power to give to you…")…p. 82
Coasting Song, A…p. 107
Coming of the New Year, The…p. 87
Cranberry Tart, The…p. 20
Dawning of the Year, The…p. 102
Day Before Christmas, The…p. 42

Dear Santa Claus, Come!...p. 48
December ("The music of the brook is hushed…") …p. 83
December ("Though in her pride young June may wear…")…p. 13
1890…p. 105
Elsie and the Year…p. 86
First Snow, The…p. 15
Gingerbread…p. 19
Grandma's Christmas, Too.…p. 80
January…p. 104
Joy to the Christmas Time…p. 62
Letter To Santa Claus, A…p. 50
Mistletoe, The…p. 30
Mistletoe Bough, The…p. 37
New Year, The…p. 101
Old and the New, The…p. 96
Old Aunt's Gift, An…p. 71
Our Christmas…p. 68
Popping Corn…p. 21
Santa Claus's Birds…p. 47
Skaters, The…p. 22
Sleigh-Bells…p. 17
Sleigh-Ride, The…p. 26
Watching for the New Year…p. 91
We Forget Hours But Remember Moments…p. 99
Welcomes and Adieus…p. 98
What the New Year Brings…p. 89

What Willie Wants…p. 44
Will He Come?…p. 52
Winter Is Coming… p. 14
Winter Morning, A…p. 24

Index of First Lines

""Ah, my life is sweet," moaned the gray Old Year…" (The Old and the New)—p. 96

"All honor to the Cranberry Tart…" (The Cranberry Tart)— p. 20

"And in the frosty season, when the sun…" (The Skaters)— p. 22

"Another year!…" (The Dawning of the Year)— p. 102

"A welcome for the New-born Year…" (Welcomes and Adieus)— p. 98

"A windy sky…" (Winter is Coming)— p. 14

"Bring ye boughs of spicy pine…" (Christmas Greens)— p. 36

"Christmas ever comes love-laden…" (A Christmas Wish)—p. 72

""Come, Elsie," said the fair young Year…" (Elsie and the Year)— p. 86

"Come, haste, let us seek it…" (A Christmas Glee)— p. 32

"Dear Santa Claus…" (What Willie Wants)— p. 44

"Dear Santa Claus, come!…" (Dear Santa Claus, Come!)— p. 48

"Dear Santa Claus keeps a bower of birds…" (Santa Claus's Birds)— p. 47

"Dear Santa Claus, please don't forget to call at our house…" (A Letter to Santa Claus)— p. 50

"Do you hear the merry bells…" (Sleigh-Bells)— p. 17

"Fear held my hand as the Old Year passed…" (At the New Year Morn)— p. 103

"From the quaint old farm-house, nestling warmly…" (A Coasting Song)— p. 107

"Had I power to give to you…" (A Christmas Wish)— p. 82

"Heap the holly! Wreath the pine!…" (A Christmas Song)— p. 39

"How does the sylvan year begin…" (The Coming of the New Year)— p. 87

"It is so tempting to know they're there…" (The Day Before Christmas)— p. 42

"I wish a merry Christmas…" (A Christmas Greeting)— p. 61

"January, crisp and clear..." (January)— p. 104

"Just when the room is getting dark..." (Popping Corn)— p. 21

"Little, bright-haired, thoughtful Florence..." (Grandma's Christmas, Too.)— p. 80

"Make glad to-night, O hearts, O hearts..." (Joy to the Christmas Time)— p. 62

"Many long, long years ago..." (An Old Aunt's Gift)— p. 71

"Mary Hanner, run this minute..." (Gingerbread)— p. 19

"Only a garland of withered leaves..." (The New Year)— p. 101

"Our Benny's new skates are a treasure..." (Baby Joe's Philosophy)— p. 79

"Over meadows, brown and sere..." (The First Snow)— p. 15

"Over the snow, over the snow..." (The Sleigh-Ride)— p. 26

"Ring! Ring!..." (Christmas Chimes)— p. 57

"Skirting close the frozen brooklet, with its mirror face of ice…" (Christmas on the Farm)— p. 59

"Small feet before the dawn of day…" (Christmas Morn)— p. 56

"The keen, clear air —the splendid sight…" (A Winter Morning)— p. 24

"The music of the brook is hushed…" (December)— p. 83

"The passing bell, for the dying year…" (Watching for the New Year)— p. 91

"The snow lies white on hill and dell…" (What the New Year Brings)— p. 89

"They are hanging the Mistletoe, bonny and bright…" (The Mistletoe Bough)— p. 37

"They come to us —they come to us…" (We Forget Hours But Remember Moments)— p. 99

"Though in her pride young June may wear…" (December)—p. 13

"Though rude winds usher thee, sweet day…" (Christmas Day)— p. 64

"Three pairs of little stockings…" (Will He Come?)— p. 52

""Time cuts down all, both great and small…" (Another Year)— p. 92

"'Tis Christmas, merry Christmas…" (Christmas Pensées)— p. 67

"Trim up the parlors, Goodwife, and make them extra-gay…" (A Christmas Party)— p. 73

"'Twas Christmas Eve, and all the land…" (Choosing the Mistletoe)— p. 34

"We didn't have much of a Christmas…" (Our Christmas)— p. 68

"What shall we give to the baby…" (Baby's Christmas Gift)— p. 78

"When Christmas time is almost here…" (The Christmas Pretender)— p. 45

"Who has the key of Christmas Land?…" (Christmas Land)— p. 66

"With Christmas cheer the hall is bright…" (The Mistletoe)— p. 30

"With song and laughter welcome to our lands…" (1890)— p. 105

FROST FARIES.

About the Editor

Sarah A. Chrisman is the author of the charming Tales of Chetzemoka historical fiction series as well as *This Victorian Life*, *Victorian Secrets*, and others. She lives in a house built in 1888, sews her own clothes, bakes her own bread in a wood-burning stove from 1901, and incorporates as many elements of Victorian culture and technology into her daily life as humanly possible. To learn more about Sarah and her books, go to www.ThisVictorianLife.com.

The Tales of Chetzemoka
By Sarah A. Chrisman

In a seaport town in the late 19th-century Pacific Northwest, a group of friends find themselves drawn together —by chance, by love, and by the marvelous changes their world is undergoing. In the process, they learn that the family we choose can be just as important as the ones we're born into. Join their adventures in *The Tales of Chetzemoka*!

http://www.thisvictorianlife.com/historical-fiction.html

Printed in Great Britain
by Amazon